D1491215

A Candle in the Dark

For Tamar

A Candle
in the Dark

Adèle Geras

Illustrated by Elsie Lennox

A & C Black · London

FLASHBACKS

All the Gold in the World · Robert Leeson
The Saga of Aslak · Susan Price
A Ghost-Light in the Attic · Pat Thomson

Published 1995 by A & C Black (Publishers) Ltd
35 Bedford Row, London WC1R 4JH

Text copyright © 1995 Adèle Geras
Illustrations copyright © 1995 Elsie Lennox

The right of Adèle Geras to be identified as author of
this work has been asserted by her in accordance
with the Copyright, Designs and Patents Act 1988.

ISBN 0-7136-4058-8

A CIP catalogue record for this book
is available from the British Library.

Photoset in Linotron Palatino by
Rowland Phototypesetting Ltd,
Bury St Edmunds, Suffolk

Printed in Great Britain by
St Edmundsbury Press Ltd,
Bury St Edmunds, Suffolk

Contents

Author's Note

Long Easterby is an imaginary village. All the characters in this book are fictional. The historical events leading up to the Kindertransports are true, and I have based the story of what happens to Clara and Maxi on real accounts.

· 1 ·

9th November, 1938

A Night of Broken Glass

Clara had never seen a grown man cry. Herr Stern, fat, bald, funny old Herr Stern from Papa's shop was weeping. He was wiping his tears away with the backs of his hands as he spoke, in just the same way Maxi did, but Maxi was four years younger than she was. Maxi was only five.

The clock chimed two. Clara had never before been awake as late as this. Frantic knocking, hammering at the door had woken her. It must have been Herr Stern. Clara crept into the salon and no one told her to go back to bed. Her mother was still dressed . . . had she not been to sleep at all? There was a pot of fresh coffee on the table. But why was Herr Stern visiting in the middle of the night?

'The shop,' Herr Stern said. 'They have smashed all the windows. They have thrown the furniture into the streets . . . it's lying upside down in the gutter. All the shops, not just ours. They are all destroyed. And they have torches . . .

fire and glass everywhere, fire and glass. In the middle of the road they have bonfires. They are burning everything: books, so many books, even the Holy Book, even the *Torah*. Nothing is sacred.' Herr Stern's voice faded almost to a whisper. 'They are marching on the synagogues. Not one brick of any synagogue in the whole of Germany will be left standing on another . . . this is what they are saying . . .'

Clara's mother, Lotte, said soothingly:

'Sit, Herr Stern. Sit down. Drink some coffee. No good will come from tears. Please, sit here.'

'But where is your husband, gnädige Frau? Where is Herr Nussbaum? That is the worst of all. They are taking away all the men they can find. Rounding them up and taking them to a camp, to a prison . . . who knows where they will take them. Who knows when they will return.'

'My husband is in Leipzig,' said Lotte.

'Thank God,' said Herr Stern and he allowed himself to be led to a chair.

Clara could see how white her mother's face was, how tightly her lips were clamped together, and how her hands trembled as she poured out the coffee. She could hear, in the distance, a rhythmic pounding that was coming nearer and nearer. I know that sound, she thought. I've heard it before. It's Them, marching. 'They' were the Nazis. Clara tried not to say that word, even to herself. It was an ugly, black little word that buzzed in her head and reminded her of spiders; the spider-symbol of the Swastika which was on every flag now, and on every street, made her feel a little ill. Nothing was the same any more, not since Herr Hitler had become Chancellor. Everything had changed. Clara remembered the first time she had read a notice on a shop window: 'Jews are not wanted as customers in this shop.' She had turned to her mother in horror.

'But this is Tante Trude's drapery! We always come here.'

'From now on,' said Lotte, 'If Trude serves us it will cause trouble for her.'

'She likes me,' Clara said. 'I know she likes me. Last time we were in the shop, she gave me nearly half a metre of pink ribbon for Angelika's petticoat. Real satin ribbon.'

'Poor Angelika!' Lotte tried to make light of it.

'Soon she will cease to be the best-dressed doll in town. Come, we will try to find a draper somewhere else.'

Everything was different. Elsa, who had been coming to the flat since Clara was a baby to help with the cleaning and the cooking, didn't come any longer. Working for Jewish families was frowned upon, and Clara had heard her father say, sadly, that soon even Nussbaum and Sons, the furniture store that had been in the family for years and years, would be theirs no longer. No Jew would be allowed to own anything.

Losing her best friend, though – that was the very worst of all. At first, when Marianne moved from her usual place in the classroom to sit beside Monika, Clara couldn't understand why.

'My father told me I mustn't sit next to you any longer,' Marianne said. 'So I can't.'

Clara walked home from school that day all by herself for the first time. A fog of tears had filled her eyes, so that she could hardly find her way. Now she went to a Jewish school and hardly ever saw Marianne. Only once, in the street, the person whom she had loved best in the world after

Mama and Papa and Maxi had crossed over to the other pavement to avoid her.

'Try not to cry when such things happen,' Clara's mother had told her. 'I know how much it must have hurt you, but don't give her the satisfaction. Pretend you don't care.'

Clara thought of these things as the noises grew louder and louder, outside in the street. Inside, there was nothing but silence. Suddenly, Mitzi, the new black-and-white kitten, raced out from behind Maxi's bedroom door and fled across the floor. She squeezed herself into the tiny gap between the bottom of the bookcase and the floor. Maxi came chasing into the salon after her, dressed in his nightclothes.

'Mama, there's shouting! Mitzi is frightened . . . she ran away . . .'

'Come and sit here next to me, Maxi, and keep very quiet till the noise is finished. Mitzi is under the bookcase. She is quite safe, liebling.'

'But why are they shouting? What are they doing? Will they come here?'

'Sssh! Sit quietly and maybe they will go soon,' said Lotte.

They *are* coming, Clara thought. They will come. We are like small animals, hiding in the forest, waiting for the hunters. I can hear them downstairs. I can hear boots on the stone steps. They are breaking everything. There was screaming now, and sobbing and howling. Clara realized she could recognize voices she knew . . . neighbours' voices. They will be here soon, she thought, and she sat with every nerve and muscle tensed, waiting for the door to crash open. Maxi covered his ears with his hands and closed his eyes.

When they came, there were three of them; three men, dressed in black and wearing peaked caps and enormous leather gloves. Clara, Lotte, Herr Stern and Maxi sat frozen with terror in their chairs.

'You will come with us,' said one of the men to Herr Stern. 'Immediately.'

'You are making a mistake,' Lotte said, 'if you think this is my husband. Can you not see how old this gentleman is? Are you dragging grandfathers away now?'

'Your husband,' said the tallest of the men in black. 'Where is he?'

'He is travelling,' said Lotte. 'On business.'

'A Jew with business?' The man laughed as though this was the funniest joke he'd heard in his life. His friends joined in the merriment.

'In that case we shall continue upstairs.'

'But not before admiring,' said the second man, 'your wonderful collection of china.' He walked over to the closed cabinet. Behind the glass-fronted doors (three panes on one side and three on the other) were the cups and plates, the jugs and small statues that Lotte loved and cared for. Once a week she took out each piece, and washed and dried it carefully before putting it back in its proper place.

'Dresden,' said the man. 'Meissen, Sèvres. I can see you are devoted to fine things.'

He spoke gently, softly. Clara was almost soothed by his smooth voice, his kind words. Then in one movement, he slammed a black-gloved fist through one of the panes in the cabinet door. The glass fell on the polished wooden floor with a silvery tinkle. After six blows from the black fist, both floor and carpet were iced with broken glass, glittering like gemstones.

'A splendid collection,' the man said again, quietly, and swept the china from the shelves. Bits of plates and jugs and cups edged with gold paint sprang and bounced in the air before falling and shattering into fragments. Clara's heart beat in her

throat. She could see, lying on the floor, one small statuette that was still unbroken. It was a shepherdess in a pink dress and a hat with blue ribbons. Please, she thought, please let him not see it. Please let him leave it where it is. The man smiled, and almost as though he could read Clara's mind, he brought the heel of his tall, black boot down on the shepherdess's face, and ground it to powder. Afterwards, Clara found a tiny porcelain hand under the rug.

'We will bid you goodnight,' said the tallest man.

Two of them had already gone, already started up the stairs to the next flat, when the third man, the only one who had not spoken a word, picked up the Menorah, the heavy, silver, nine-branched candelabra which stood on the sideboard.

'What is this?' he asked. 'Is this a religious object?'

'Yes,' said Lotte, squaring her shoulders and looking into the man's eyes. 'We will need it to light candles when Hannukah comes.'

The man in black tossed the Menorah into the air. It flew from his hands as though it were weightless. Up and up in a curve across the room it went, towards the window. It sailed through the glass, dragging the curtain behind it. The sound the lace made as it tore was like a shriek; the noise of the silver exploding through the glass was the sound of the end of the world.

After the men had gone, no one spoke for a long time. Then Lotte looked at Clara and said:

'Tomorrow, we start English lessons. I will begin to make arrangements. I will not permit my children to live in this hell. Now Clara, fetch a broom from the kitchen, please . . . and you, Maxi, you must help as well. We will make the floor safe for when Mitzi decides to come out.'

Maxi took his hands away from his ears and began to cry.

· 2 ·

10th December, 1938

Long Easterby, Leicestershire

Phyllis Baird and her friend Eileen Forrester were bored with hopscotch. They huddled together in the shelter of the playground wall, hiding from the wind and waiting for Miss Peabody to ring the bell, so that they could go back into the warm classroom.

'Our German girl and her brother,' said Phyllis, 'are getting here on Monday. Daddy's going to meet the boat from Holland. I do hope she's nice.'

'Will she speak English, do you think?' asked Eileen. She was a tall, well-built girl with pink cheeks and curly hair and teeth that stuck out a little. 'It won't be any fun having someone to stay who can't talk to you, will it?'

'Her mother's been teaching her. Daddy said so. I expect she'll know some words. Anyway, she and her brother are coming to school, so I should think Miss Pea will help them.'

'Did you invite them?' Eileen wanted to know. Secretly, she thought it was a bit peculiar, Phyllis coming over all interested in foreigners, and Germans at that. She said:

'My Dad says there's going to be a war. My Dad says Germany's going to be the enemy before you can say "boo" to a goose. He said so.'

'Clara and her brother are Jewish. Their mother used to be a penfriend of Daddy's, ages ago,' said Phyllis, saying Clara in the German way, with the 'ar' rhyming with 'far', just as her father had said it. As soon as Eileen answered, Phyllis could see she was intent on being difficult. She deliberately said the name in the English way, to rhyme with 'wearer'.

'Clara isn't an orphan, is she?'

'No,' said Phyllis, 'but things are very bad for anyone Jewish in Germany, and it's dangerous to stay there, so there's a special committee now that helps Jewish children come here, where they'll be safe.' She knew the name given to the plan. It was called the Kindertransport. 'Kinder' was German for 'children'. She kept all this to herself, however, knowing very well how Eileen would scoff at her attempt at a foreign . . . an enemy . . . language.

'I wouldn't go,' said Eileen, 'and that's flat. I wouldn't leave my Mum and Dad and Long Easterby and go traipsing off to another country where I didn't know a soul, would you?'

Phyllis thought for a moment. She was a small, sandy-haired, short-sighted girl. She wore spectacles with blue plastic frames and was devoted to Eileen. She didn't know why Eileen had chosen her as a special friend, but she was very grateful for the honour. Every girl in the class wanted to be best friends with Eileen. In the end she said:

'I might if it was dangerous to stay.'

'I don't expect it's *that* dangerous,' Eileen continued. 'My Mum says you can depend on Jewish people to exaggerate.'

Phyllis bit her tongue to stop her answer flying out of her mouth. She'd nearly said that Eileen's mum was as bad as Horrible Hitler, then, and anyway what did she know about Jewish people? Had she ever met one? Even though Eileen was her best friend, she could be annoying and spiteful sometimes, so Phyllis only said:

'You *will* be nice to her, Eileen, won't you? You will try to be friends?'

'I'll see,' said Eileen, 'it depends on what she's like. Come on, there's Miss Pea. Bell's going to ring any minute.'

She set off running across the playground, with Phyllis following more slowly behind her.

Miss Peabody had the kind of figure ladies' magazines called 'comfortable'. She was round all over. 'Like a cottage loaf,' said Eileen. 'More like a potato than a pea. Potatobody . . . that's what she should be called.' When Phyllis told her mother about this nickname, Gillian Baird had sniffed.

'A case of the pot calling the kettle black, that is,' she said. 'Eileen is a big girl, and her Mum is not exactly a sylph, is she?'

Phyllis giggled. Perhaps Potatobody was too much of a mouthful. In any case, the nickname had never caught on, and the teacher was known to the whole village as Miss Pea. She taught the older children, while skinny, wispy Mrs Goodison was in charge of the Infants. The school was very small. It had only two classrooms, an assembly hall and a playground, shaded by trees growing in the churchyard next door.

'Now, children,' Miss Peabody said, when everyone had settled down. 'I shall want those of you who have speaking parts in the Nativity play to stay behind for half an hour today, and again on Monday. Some bits were very ragged on Wednesday . . . the Angel appearing to the shepherds was all over the place.'

'Please, Miss Peabody,' said Phyllis, 'may I be excused rehearsal on Monday? I have to go home because our German visitors are arriving that day.'

'Of course, dear,' said Miss Peabody. 'I forgot,

I'm so sorry. How dreadfully sad it all is! Your mother was telling me all about it after church last week.' She clapped her hands.

'Children,' she said, 'next week we will be joined by two German children, Clara and Max Nussbaum. Clara is nine, and Max is five. You are to make them feel very welcome, and help them in every possible way.'

Phyllis was relieved to hear Miss Peabody pronouncing Clara's name correctly. She glanced at Eileen, who was staring out of the window, pretending not to pay attention. Ginger Roberts put his hand up:

'Please, Miss,' he said, 'will the new kids be in the play? In the Nativity play?'

'They're Jewish,' said Eileen. 'Jewish people don't believe in Jesus, so how can they be in a Nativity play?'

'That will do, Eileen,' said Miss Peabody. 'Jesus Christ himself was Jewish, as I'm sure you know. If being in a Nativity play will make life pleasant for our visitors, and if they would like to be in it, I shall do my best to accommodate them. And how do you spell "accommodate", children?

Does anyone know? I shall put it up on the black-board with some other words, and you will all learn them for a test on Monday.'

She took up a fresh piece of white chalk, and wrote:

'Accommodate. Transportation. Refugee. Tolerance. Committee. Belief.'

Then she turned back to face the children.

'When you have finished copying those words into your notebooks, please turn to page 63 of your arithmetic books. This morning we are going to grapple with fractions.'

· 3 ·

9th–13th December, 1938

Kindertransport

'Clara . . . Clara are you asleep? May I come in?'

'I'm not asleep,' Clara said. 'It's difficult. I keep thinking about tomorrow.'

Lotte sat down at the foot of her daughter's bed. Clara could see how tired she looked, even though the only light in the room came from the corridor.

'It's about tomorrow that I want to talk to you, Clara.' Lotte sighed. 'I wish your father were here. I wish he could see you and Maxi before you go . . . have you got the postcard?'

Clara pulled out the thin, white rectangle from its hiding-place under the pillow. This was the message her father had sent her from Dachau, the camp to which he had been taken. Clara had thought Papa was safe in Leipzig, but the Nazis had found him and taken him away. There was nothing in the card about what the camp was like, but he said that he was well, and would be home soon. *'You must be brave and good,'* Papa went on, *'and look after Maxi, and we will all meet again in England.'* Clara wondered if he was lying to make her feel better. She had heard the grown-ups talking in hushed voices about the camps. People were badly treated there; they were beaten and even killed sometimes. Clara tried not to think about it, and during the day that was easy. At night, though, she sometimes dreamed of her father dressed in rags and with his face as thin and pale as a living skull.

'You understand,' Lotte said, 'why we are sending you to England, you and Maxi?'

'Yes, Mama, of course I do.'

'However terrible things have been here, they may get worse. Much, much worse. It frightens me to imagine how bad things might be in the future. Still, they say that anyone who can produce travel documents, an exit visa and a passport, will be released from the camp, and of course I am doing all that I can. When your father comes home, he and I will make every effort to come to England as soon as possible. We will only be separated for a few months . . . maybe only a few weeks. I want you to remember that when you feel sad or homesick. We will think of you every minute, and we would love you to be happy. It would make everything much easier for us if we knew you and Maxi were . . . all right.'

Clara said: 'Of course, we will be fine. I know how lucky we are. I even know how to speak a little English, and we know where we are going. Very few children are so fortunate. And you've prepared envelopes and I will write and tell you how lovely it is in England.'

'Good girl. You are my good, brave girl, and you will look after Maxi who doesn't really know what is happening . . . We are all frightened, Clara. Sometimes I do not know if I can get through the day without showing how frightened I am; without crying and breaking down, but I try, and you must too. Try hard, very hard not to cry.'

Lotte kissed her daughter and left the room. Clara heard her sighing as she closed the door, and knew that she was not supposed to. Her mother pretended so hard to be cheerful all the time for her sake, and for Maxi's. Clara felt tears sliding out of the corners of her eyes in spite of all her bright words.

'I'm not crying,' she whispered aloud. 'I'm not.' She sat up in bed and rubbed her face with a corner of the quilt. This time tomorrow, she thought, we will be on the train. She looked around her bedroom. There was the dark shape of her cupboard, and on the chair beside the door, her suitcase was ready. Angelika was too big to fit into it.

'Leave her with me,' Mama had said, 'and I will bring her to you in England, I promise. Meanwhile, she will keep me company when you are far away.'

'Tell me about the train!' Maxi asked on the way to the station. 'I want to go on the train. Is it a big train? Will it go fast?'

Maxi was excited. Clara was relieved that his chatter kept Mama busy. If she was answering all his questions, she wouldn't have time to think about saying goodbye. Clara felt as though all the tears she wanted to shed had gathered into a lump at the back of her throat. She found it hard to swallow, and even harder to speak. The little suitcase she was carrying dragged at her fingers. In her shoulder bag, she knew, were all the papers she and Maxi needed, and their passports, stamped with a 'J' for 'Jude'. Jew. I mustn't lose the bag, Clara thought. Our money and Papa's postcard from the camp and some photographs are in there as well. Even if I fall asleep on the train, I must hold on to the bag. I must hold on to it all the time.

'Look at the children, Mama!' Maxi cried when he saw the crowds on the platform. 'Are they coming on the train too?'

'Yes, darling,' said Mama. 'They are all going to England. That man over there, and that lady . . . they will be on the train as well, in case you need help. They are from the committee that looks after refugees.'

There was a cardboard label around the neck of each child. Some were already wailing, clinging to their mothers' coats. Clara saw that parents were crying too, their mouths open, their eyes red. She glanced at her own mother. Lotte stood quietly, smartly dressed in her best coat with the velvet collar and her red hat with the black veil. This is how she wants me to think of her, Clara realized. Looking beautiful, looking happy. It was hard to see Lotte's eyes properly in the dim light of the station, and under the veil. Were they glittery with tears?

'Are you all right, Mama?' Clara asked.

'I am glad that you and Maxi have this chance to be free . . . to be away from here.'

Policemen in black began to shout; children and parents surged toward the train.

'Let's get in!' Maxi shouted. 'Let's find a seat. We can wave at Mama from the window.'

'Go,' said Lotte. She kissed Maxi, who seemed hardly to notice. He scrambled on to the train as fast as he could. Then she turned to kiss Clara.

'Be brave,' she said, and her voice sounded strangely thick and muffled.

'Look after Maxi. He will be sad, later, when all the excitement of being on a train wears off. Write to me.'

Clara knew she couldn't speak, not even one word. If I open my mouth, she thought, all the tears that are squashed together in the back of my throat will spill out, like a waterfall and drown my mother. Instead, she clung to Lotte, squeezing her hard, hard around the neck. Then, unable to look at her any more, wanting only to be gone, and for the saying goodbye to be over, Clara stumbled on to the train and went to look for Maxi.

'Here, Clara, here I am,' he called to her as she looked into the first compartment. 'I'm right by the window.'

Clara nodded and went to sit beside her brother, whose nose was pressed flat against the glass. Other children pushed into the remaining seats. Clara noticed a girl of about twelve, holding the hand of a toddler who couldn't have been older than three. There were some boys, but Clara was too busy looking out of the window to pay them any attention.

Lotte and the other parents had been pushed back behind a barrier. Every hand that Clara could see was waving. There were thousands and thousands of them. Even through the glass, she could hear the wailing. Crying and sobbing coming from somewhere behind her. I wish the train would start, Clara thought. I wish it would go.

'We're moving,' Maxi shouted. There was a hiss of steam and the train shuddered and began to pull out of the station. Clara made sure she was smiling as she waved goodbye. Lotte smiled back as though this were a happy day. Clara watched her mother's figure growing smaller and smaller. She could still see the red hat when Lotte's face had become too tiny to recognize. Of course, Clara thought, that is why she wore it.

Suddenly, a mother with tears pouring out of her eyes broke free of the barrier and began to run alongside the train, holding her hands out as though she could grab her disappearing child, and snatch her back, back into her arms and hold her there. Clara turned away, unable to bear the sight. I will not cry, she thought. I will be as brave as Mama.

They had been on the train for only half an hour when Maxi turned to Clara and said:

'I like this train, but I want to go home now. Can we go home now, Clara? I want to see Mama. I want to see Mitzi.'

When she thought about it afterwards, it seemed to Clara that the time she and Maxi spent on the train to Holland was like a dream, or an old-fashioned flickering film at the cinema where images followed one after another before you had time to make sense of them.

All night long, she was halfway between sleeping and waking. Maxi had cried and cried, and she had comforted him with tales of all the wonderful things there would be in England. What if all her stories turned out to be untrue? Maxi would cry all over again, but by then Mr and Mrs Baird would be able to help console him.

The metal clack and hum of the wheels on the track was like an accompaniment to the chatter of the children in the compartment. The girl in charge of the baby was called Eva.

'This isn't my sister,' Eva told Clara. 'She's a neighbour's baby. The mother begged me to take her. I didn't really want to, but what could I say? I couldn't say no, and now she's mine to look after.' Eva sighed. 'It'll make things difficult in England. They say it's harder to find a sponsor if there's two of you and you don't want to be separated.'

Most of the children, Clara discovered, were going to live in a holiday camp by the sea until homes could be found for them.

'They've got it all ready for us,' said one boy. 'A member of the Refugee Committee told me. We will have lessons in English, and people will come and choose us to live in their houses.'

Clara thought: but what if your friends are chosen and you are not? What if you're chosen by a family you don't like? At least she knew a little about where she and Maxi would be. They were lucky.

All through the night, every few hours, there

were visits from German guards. Only the very youngest of the children stayed asleep when they appeared. Every time she saw a swastika or a black hat, Clara looked down, almost unable to breathe. What if their papers were inspected? What if something about them wasn't quite right? She and Maxi might be turned back, might not be allowed to escape.

Dawn came at last. Out of the window, Clara could see that the countryside looked flatter. Soon, soon, they would be out of Germany and safe in Holland.

After an inspection by the Dutch Customs, the train slid into the station, puffing blue-grey clouds of steam. Every child who could reach a window was leaning out of it, and smiling and shouting. The platform was crowded; everyone in Holland, it seemed to Clara, was there to welcome them.

'Look!' said Maxi. 'There's food, and people are having drinks.'

As they climbed down from the train, the children were given chocolate and lemonade and best of all, thick slices of soft, white bread. Clara and Maxi waited for theirs. A kind lady, wearing an apron over her coat, gave Maxi an extra bar of chocolate. She smiled at Clara and spoke in German:

'He looks the same age as my grandson . . . and you, will you have some more lemonade?'

Clara nodded and thanked the lady. Maxi wanted to stay with her. He clung to her skirts. In the end, the Dutch lady herself persuaded him to follow Clara out of the station. They were almost the last to make their way down to the dock. Just as they were leaving, Clara felt a hand pulling at her sleeve.

'Miss . . . little Miss . . .'

Clara turned. An old man stood at her elbow, holding a small ragdoll. Clara saw immediately how pretty she was, and with what love she had been made. Oh, Angelika, Clara thought, I wish I could have brought you with me. Only the voice of the old man speaking to her in German stopped her from crying. He said:

'She is for you. This is a small gift for you. Please take.'

Clara held the doll close. 'Thank you,' she said. 'Thank you . . .' and then a member of the

Committee came and took her by the hand, to hurry her and Maxi towards the ship.

Clara named the ragdoll Rosa, because of the pattern of little red roses on the material of her dress. She tried as hard as she could to think about Rosa, and not about the huge, black bulk of the ship that was to take them to England. How was it going to remain afloat when it was so heavy, and when there were so many people on it? Clara worried about this until she saw that all the sailors were walking quite normally around the decks, as though they expected the ship to stay bobbing about on the surface for ever. Perhaps it would, but Clara was unconvinced for the first few hours on board, and clutched Rosa for comfort.

Maxi liked the ship, and wanted to go and look at the engines, but the sea was not what he had expected.

'Why isn't it blue?' he asked Clara over and over again.

'I don't know,' she shouted in the end. 'I don't know why . . . you always expect me to know everything! Go and ask someone else for a change.'

Maxi did. He asked every single person he saw, and at last he told Clara:

'A boy told me why. I know now. The sea is only blue when the sky is blue. There.'

Maxi looked so happy to have learned this, that Clara hugged him.

'I'm sorry I shouted at you,' she said. 'You're a clever boy to have found out the answer.'

All through the night, Clara lay in her narrow bunk and clung to Rosa. The ship was heaving and groaning its way through the waves, creaking and shuddering and rolling in a way that terrified Clara and most of the other children in the cabin, and made some people dreadfully sick.

It was still dark the next morning when the ship docked, but Clara was happy to see dry land. What did it matter what England was like, she thought, as long as it wasn't the sea? All she asked of this new country was that it should stay still and not move around under her feet.

· 4 ·

13th December, 1938

A Letter Home

Clara picked up her pencil and began to write in German:

Darling Mama,

This is my first proper letter from England. I hope you have received all the postcards, telling you about the journey. Everything happens so quickly that it is hard to know where to begin.

It is a treat to write in German after all the English I have been trying to speak and also to read and write. Miss Peabody is the kind teacher in the school here. She came to meet me and Maxi, and to tell us that we are welcome in her school. She will give me extra lessons in conversation. Maxi is learning English very quickly. In a few weeks he will speak like an English boy. I speak to him in German, because it's easier. Please write and tell me if I should. Maybe I should give him extra practice in English.

We are very happy with Mr and Mrs Baird.

Clara sucked the end of her pencil, and looked out of the window. How could she *show* the Bairds to her mother? How could she tell her everything? Mr Baird ('Call me Uncle Peter,' he had said within seconds of meeting her and Maxi) was big and hairy and wore a fawn-coloured cardigan with brown buttons. He spoke to them all the way home, as though he were frightened of silences. He was practising his terrible German, he said, and made Maxi laugh at all his mistakes. Clara thought that without Maxi the long journey from Harwich to Long Easterby would have been dreadful, but her little brother asked question after question, and he and Uncle Peter spent most of the time chatting about locomotives. Phyllis and Auntie Gillian (Mrs Baird) were waiting at the house. Auntie Gillian was thin and brown. The house was brown and fawn, too, and the furniture was upholstered in a shade of green that was nearly khaki. Auntie Gillian looked embarrassed. Clara could see that she wanted to hug them, but somehow her arms remained fixed to her sides, and all she said was: 'You must be very tired. Come in and sit down and have a cup of tea.'

The tea was sweet and milky. Maxi liked it, but Clara had longed, suddenly, for Mama's hot chocolate with whipped cream on top, or milky coffee. Her cheeks had ached all that first night, from smiling so brightly.

Phyllis was very quiet to begin with. Auntie Gillian had taken Maxi off to have a bath, and left the girls alone together in the nursery. There was a small bed in there for Clara, and a camp bed for Maxi. At first, neither she nor Phyllis could think of a word to say. Then Clara started to take her few belongings out of her suitcase, and when Phyllis saw Rosa, she began to talk:

'Oh, what a lovely ragdoll! Has she got a name?'

'Rosa.'

'That's nice. I've got lots of dolls. Would you like to see them?'

Clara nodded.

'Put your things in the chest-of-drawers, then, and come to my room. It's just across the landing. I'll go and get the dolls ready.'

Clara understood the invitation, but wondered about the 'chest-something' Phyllis had mentioned. She had spoken very quickly . . . maybe Clara had not heard her properly. Wasn't 'chest' the word for the front bit of the body? Clara sighed and put the clothes away in the drawers.

Phyllis had lined up all her dolls on the bed.

'This is Daisy, Suzy, Anna, Blossom and Bunty. Daisy is my best. Have you got lots of dolls in Germany?'

'I have a doll like this . . .' Clara held her hands apart to show how big Angelika was, but had no words to tell Phyllis how beautifully blue her eyes were; how prettily they closed when she was put down to rest; how long her eyelashes were; how elegantly she was dressed.

'Gosh!' Phyllis said. 'That's jolly big. Wait till you see Eileen's dolls' house. Eileen's my best friend. You'll meet her at school.'

Clara nodded, but could think of nothing to say. Phyllis went on:

'I like your brother.'

Clara smiled. 'Thank you,' she said. 'You are very kind. He is much talking. Much noise.'

Phyllis giggled. Clara thought: perhaps we are going to be friends after all.

Now, Clara remembered how long it had taken them to fall asleep that first night in England.

'I don't like the bit at the top of the stairs,' Maxi had whispered. 'It's dark there. Maybe there are bad things hiding . . .'

'Nonsense,' Clara had said. 'There are no bad things here. This is England. We are safe.'

When Maxi's breathing became snuffly and snorey, Clara knew he was asleep. She had lain awake, staring at the dark. Auntie Gillian had come in to tuck them up, hours ago it seemed, and to say good night, but she hadn't kissed them. After she had gone, Clara had whispered aloud in German:

'I want my mother. How can I sleep without her kiss?' Two fat tears had slid out of the corners of her eyes, before she could stop them. Thinking about that night made Clara feel sad all over again, so she blinked quickly and carried on with her letter.

They have asked us to call them Uncle Peter and Auntie Gillian. The house is very big. It has a name, Yew Tree House, and four bedrooms upstairs. Maxi and I are in a bedroom called the nursery. There is an old rocking horse in there, and some toys no one plays with any more. Phyllis Baird is six months older than me. She is nice, but quite shy. It is sometimes hard to know what to say to her. She and her friend Eileen took me and Maxi for a walk yesterday, to show us the village. Mama, it is very small. You can walk all round it in half an hour. There are only four streets with houses and gardens, and all the streets lead to the village green, which is like a piece of grass with a pond in the middle. There are ducks on the pond. Maxi liked the ducks. He also liked a cat we saw and wanted to follow it and pick it up and bring it back to Yew Tree House. There is an inn called The Rambling Rose, and a shop and a post office and a church. The school is next to the church. That is all there is. There are no cafés, no parks, no theatres, no big shops, and not very many lights. At night everything is dark and silent. It is very peaceful but I miss the noises and the lights. I miss you and Papa very much, and wait for the day when you will come here to England.

I miss the food we used to have. Here there is funny boiled tasteless cabbage and thin gravy, but Phyllis gave me wonderful chocolate called Mars. For tea, there is plum jam, which is delicious. Last night we had rice pudding. Maxi liked it but I hated it. Have you ever had rice pudding? It has horrible burnt skin on top. I felt I had to eat a little, so that Auntie Gillian wouldn't be offended, but I was nearly sick. I hope we don't have it too often.

Miss Peabody told us that the children in the school are putting on a play for Christmas. She asked me if we would like to join in, even though we are Jewish and don't celebrate Christmas. I said I would let her know. I tried to explain to her that although we are Jewish, we are not a very religious family, and that we always enjoyed the preparations and ceremony of Christmas, as well as those of Hannukah . . . Do you remember how we used to spend Christmas Day all together at Marianne's house, long ago before everything became horrible? I don't know what to do, Mama. I think that not to join in would seem rude, but I don't want anyone to think that I'm not properly Jewish any more; that I've turned into a Christian. God wouldn't think that, would he? And Maxi loves dressing-up. I don't want to stop him joining in the fun. I wish you were here so that I could talk to you about it. Please write to us soon. We long for your letters.

Hugs and kisses and lots and lots of love from us both.

Clara

· 5 ·
15th December, 1938
The First Day at School

Before Clara and Maxi came to Long Easterby, Phyllis had thought and thought about what they would be like. Her notion of a German girl was based on the picture decorating the cover of *Heidi*, one of her favourite books. Phyllis knew that Heidi was Swiss, but she wasn't sure exactly where one country ended and another began. In spite of Miss Peabody's best efforts in Geography lessons, Phyllis thought that German people and Swiss people were probably quite similar. Clara, she decided, would wear a blouse with puffed-out sleeves, and over it, a green pinafore laced up at the front. Maxi would probably, Phyllis thought, be wearing leather trousers with a dungaree-like bib, and a jaunty little hat.

When Clara arrived, Phyllis saw that she was dark, and had long plaits hanging neatly down her back. She wore a brown woollen coat over a dark red dress with a white collar. Her ankle socks were very white, even after a long journey, and her shoes were shiny brown leather. She had the brownest and most wide-open eyes Phyllis had ever seen, and even though she was shy and couldn't speak English well yet, she appeared very grown-up. She was obviously what Eileen called 'a London sort of person'; someone you could never imagine tramping through the mud in wellington boots, or climbing trees, or skipping across stepping stones in the stream.

Maxi was dark too, but rounder and smaller and altogether more cuddly than his sister. He was also noisier and bouncier and Phyllis loved him from the very first moment she saw him, in the same way that she would have loved a cheerful little puppy, if her mother had allowed her to have one.

Now, taking Clara and Maxi to school for the first time, she felt nervous.

'Hold my hand, Maxi,' she said as they walked through the village, 'and be a good boy.'

To Clara she said:

'I like your hair ribbons.'

'Thank you,' Clara answered. She had worn her best blue ribbons in honour of her first day in an English school.

Phyllis knew Clara was probably anxious too, but didn't quite know what to say to cheer her up. Instead, she chatted to Maxi as they walked through the frosty morning. 'We've got a cat at school, Maxi. He's called Watson. Can you say "Watson", Maxi?'

'Watson!' Maxi cried. 'Watson cat!'

'That's right . . . clever boy. A big, fat, gingery old Watson cat.'

Maxi thought this was very funny, and began to pull Phyllis along.

'Want cat!' he said. 'Come, Phyllis . . . come, Clara.' Clara smiled too. It was hard not to smile at Maxi, but she said something to him in German.

'I tell him: be good. Be quiet,' she explained to Phyllis.

'Oh, Mrs Goodison will look after him, don't worry. She'll think he's a proper little duck, just like I do, don't I, Maxi? Don't I think you're a little duck?'

'Quack!' said Maxi obligingly.

Clara said something to Maxi in German and pulled him to her side. To Phyllis she said, 'I am telling him he must listen to what *I* say. He must be good.'

Phyllis looked slightly surprised. Then she replied, 'Let's take Maxi to meet Mrs Goodison and after that we'll come back and I'll introduce you to everybody.'

The children went into school, past the cloakroom and along the short corridor to the infants' classroom.

Luckily, Watson the cat was sleeping on Mrs Goodison's chair when they arrived. Maxi was perfectly happy to leave Clara and Phyllis and sit at a little desk and wait for Watson to wake up.

'Don't you worry about your brother, dear,' Mrs Goodison said to Clara. 'We'll take care of him.' To Maxi she said:

'Just give him a little stroke on the back, lovey. You can play with him again later on, when he's not so sleepy.' Maxi did exactly as he was told.

'Isn't your brother clever?' Phyllis said as she and Clara walked back to the juniors' playground. 'He understands every word.'

Eileen and some of the other girls were waiting in the shelter of the wall. Phyllis could feel all their eyes turned on her and on Clara, and even though she knew that it was mainly Clara who was being stared at, she, too, could sense the sharpness of gazes that took in every detail of Clara's appearance and manner; looks that might very well decide whether Clara was liked or not, even before she opened her mouth.

'This is Clara Nussbaum, everybody,' Phyllis said. 'Clara, this is Eileen Forrester, and Monica Evans, and Peggy White and Mary Cranshaw. They're my friends.' Clara nodded and smiled and held out a hand to Eileen. She said:

'I am happy to meet you.'

Eileen glanced down at the outstretched hand and decided to ignore it.

'How do you do?' she said and turned to Phyllis. 'You never said she spoke English so well.'

Clara said:

'I learn English for one month. I speak not very well.'

'A jolly sight better than we speak German,'

said Eileen, and whispered something to Monica. Phyllis couldn't hear what the private remark was, but she could guess. It was probably something about no sensible person wanting to speak German anyway.

Eileen turned back to Clara.

'Say some German words, Clara,' she said. 'Let's hear what it sounds like.' Phyllis winced. Why *wouldn't* Eileen say the name properly? It wasn't difficult. She was just about to tell Clara that she didn't have to do any such thing, but it was too late; she'd already started speaking. The other girls listened. Eileen giggled a little, and the others shuffled their feet.

'What did all that mean?' Monica asked.

'It is a poem,' said Clara.

Miss Peabody came out of the classroom and rang the bell for the first lesson. Everyone lined up in the playground, ready to file into school.

'Was it really a poem?' Phyllis whispered to Clara.

'No,' Clara whispered back. 'I tell her she is a rude girl. She expects Jewish girl to be not like English girl. She is looking for something to hate.

This I tell her.'

Phyllis felt worried. What if Eileen and Clara really did dislike each one another? What could she do about it? Should she say something to Eileen? Or tell Clara not to be so prickly? In the end, she said, 'I'm sure Eileen won't hate you. Why ever should she?'

Clara said nothing. She swung her plaits back over her shoulders and walked quickly into school.

Maxi thought that Mrs Goodison's classroom was the best place he'd been in since coming to England. It wasn't as good as home. Home was the most wonderful place in the world, but Clara said they couldn't go back there for a long time. Maxi thought about home a lot. At night he closed his eyes and pretended he was in his own bed, under the feather quilt. Mama had just kissed him good night. Mitzi was curled up at the foot of the bed, and he was falling asleep . . . Sometimes Maxi really *did* fall asleep, but when he didn't, then he felt full of tears that just had to come out, and he started to cry. Maybe one day, Maxi thought, we'll go back there, but not tomorrow. The bad men who came in the night and smashed up everybody's house might come again, Clara said. Maxi thought: if they came again, maybe they would take us away, me and Clara, to a horrible place, like the place where Papa was, and that's why Mama has sent us here, where everyone speaks English. Mama said she and Papa would come. Maxi sighed. Clara knew many things, but he kept asking her and asking her: 'When will Mama and Papa come?' and all she could say was: 'I don't know.' Maybe Mama and Papa would bring Mitzi when they came. Clara, when he asked her about this, told him no animals could come to England, and Mitzi would have to stay behind. What would happen to her then? Who would feed her? Maxi knew his mother wouldn't just leave his little kitten all by herself with no one to look after her.

The teacher, Mrs Goodison, was very kind, Maxi thought. She let him sit next to Watson, and stroke him. She said to the class:

'Children, this is Maxi Nussbaum, who comes all the way from Germany, which is a very long

way away. Please look after him, and speak slowly because he is just learning how to speak English. Stand up, please, Maxi.'

Maxi stood up.

'Say: "Good morning, children,"' said Mrs Goodison.

'Good morning, children,' said Maxi.

'That's very good indeed, Maxi!' Mrs Goodison beamed at him. 'Now, what do we say, children?'

The whole class smiled at Maxi:

'Good morning, Maxi!' they said.

It was warm in the classroom. There were pictures of birds and animals on the walls. First, the children practised writing their letters, then they all wrote numbers. When reading time came, Mrs Goodison said:

'You sit there quietly with Watson, Maxi, while I hear these children read, and I'll find you a special book to look at till it's time for songs and stories.'

Maxi didn't think the book was special at all. Perhaps he would have sat and looked at it all the same, if only Watson hadn't chosen to leave the classroom, just as Mrs Goodison was busy dealing with Bobby Grantley. Maxi decided to follow the cat.

Maxi's favourite game in all the world was pretending to be a cat. It had started when Mitzi was tiny. Maxi used to curl up and pretend to sleep on the rug, right next to her. Clara would say:

'What ever are you doing, Maxi?' and Maxi's answer was always the same:

'I'm playing Be-Cats!' he would say, and begin to clean his face with a curled-up hand, copying what he had seen Mitzi doing.

Watson wasn't a kitten. Watson was elderly; a huge, slow, heavy sort of cat, and he set off down the corridor towards the cloakroom, with Maxi pretending to be huge and slow and heavy behind him. Watson stopped to sniff at coats and boots, and so did Maxi. Watson investigated the dark spaces behind the pipes, hoping for spiders, and Maxi looked in there as well. Unlike Watson, he hoped for no spiders, because he didn't like the way their legs waved about.

Watson stood at the door for a moment, and then set off across the deserted playground. Maxi followed, not even noticing how cold it was, thrilled by the adventure he was having. Where would Watson take him? Perhaps the cat would walk all the way to Yew Tree House, and stay there for ever to keep Maxi company. Watson could come up those dark stairs with him, and help him not to be frightened. He would, he

decided, tell the cat all about Mitzi and how he was longing to see her again.

Maxi didn't notice time going by. Watson had found his way into the churchyard, and after exploring the moss and ivy on some of the oldest graves, had decided that walking was over for the day, and settled himself on one of the flat tombstones. Maxi sat down next to him. Watson half-closed his eyes; so did Maxi. Watson licked his front paws. Maxi put out a tongue and licked one of his fingers. It didn't taste very nice, so he stopped. Watson carried on until his paws were thoroughly clean, and then he rested his head on them and closed his eyes for a proper sleep. Maxi sighed. It was too cold to sleep. Maybe he should go and find his coat. He didn't exactly know the way back to school, without Watson to guide him. He had no idea how long Watson would stay asleep on the tombstone. Now that there was no cat purring to comfort him, Maxi suddenly felt all alone, and more frightened than he had ever felt before. What if no one found him there? What if Watson stayed asleep for hours and hours and it grew dark? There might be scary noises from the tombstones. Maybe Maxi would have to stay in the churchyard all night with no food . . . in the cold and the dark with no one to speak to . . . no Clara . . . no Phyllis . . . nobody. Maxi opened his mouth and started wailing:

'Claa-rr-aa!' he cried. 'Clara, where are you? Clara?' He listened for an answer, and there, like a miracle, was Clara's voice, shouting back in German: 'Maxi, where are you? Tell me where you are . . .' and Phyllis's voice shouting as well, only in English: 'Maxi . . . we're coming. Tell us where you are, Maxi!'

'I'm in the churchyard!' Maxi shouted in German. 'I'm in the middle of all the tombstones!'

The girls came running towards him across the churchyard lawn. Clara was shouting and crying at the same time. Maxi had never seen his sister looking so upset.

'Maxi,' she cried, 'I was so worried . . . I thought . . . I thought . . .'

'I'm here,' Maxi said. 'I went for a walk with Watson.'

'I know you're here.' Clara hugged Maxi with one arm, and wiped her eyes with the back of her other hand. 'But I thought you were lost. Please never do such a thing again.'

'You're very naughty, Maxi,' Phyllis told him. 'Clara was so worried about you. She burst into tears in front of everyone.'

Maxi looked up at his sister. Her eyes were red and swollen.

'I'm sorry,' he said in German. 'I was playing Be-Cats. I won't do it again.'

Clara smiled. 'It's all right. I've found you now. Mrs Goodison wants you to be a lamb, not a cat. All the infants are going to be sheep and lambs.' She turned to Phyllis and said in English: 'I tell him about the Nativity play. I say: does he wish a lamb to be?'

'Yes!' said Maxi. 'I will play Be-Lambs!'

· 6 ·

Sunday, 18th December, 1938

Rehearsing for the Play

Everyone was in the hall, rehearsing the Nativity play. Miss Peabody clapped her hands:

'Come along now, please, Multitude of the Heavenly Host! Put a little more life into it! I know there are only six of you, but still . . . you really must sound more enthusiastic than that. Let's just have the carol once more, and then you may all go home and rest before tomorrow.'

Mrs Goodison attacked the piano and the Multitudes began to sing *Hark, the herald Angels!*

Phyllis and Clara sat on the floor and watched. Maxi was with the infants on one side of the stage. They were all a little restless. They'd been prancing and making lamb noises for ages now, and most of them wanted to stop and go home for tea. Eileen, who was the Chief Angel, had done her speech about finding the Babe wrapped in swaddling clothes and lying in a manger, and was beginning to fidget. Phyllis had nothing to do in this scene. She was the Innkeeper's Wife, and she only had two lines. Her best line was:

'We could let them have the stable, dear. As it's so cold and she's expecting a baby,' and she had made Clara listen to how she said it over and over again.

At last, Miss Pea was satisfied with the Heavenly Host. She thanked all the children, and after a while the hall was empty, except for Phyllis, Clara, Maxi and Eileen. Clara was going to practise her song, and Maxi and Phyllis were waiting for her. Eileen was there, too, because after they'd taken Maxi home, Phyllis and Clara were going to her house to play with her dolls.

'Are you ready, Clara dear?' said Miss Pea. Clara nodded. She stepped on to the stage and Mrs Goodison began to play the introduction to *Silent Night*. Clara sang it in German, but Phyllis thought that didn't matter a bit, as everyone knew the carol so well. She closed her eyes and listened. Clara sounded exactly like a proper angel. Miss Pea should have had her singing on her own, instead of the silly old Heavenly Host, who were always out of tune. When Clara had finished, Miss Pea said:

'That's lovely, dear. It'll be a fine way to start the play. I'll just say a few words of introduction, and then it'll be your turn. Now off you all go and have a good rest. Tomorrow will be a busy day.'

Eileen had the biggest and most beautifully-furnished dolls' house in the village.

'My Dad made it for me,' she said. 'Did you have a dolls' house in Germany, Clara?'

'No,' said Clara, 'but I have a big doll. Angelika. Very pretty. This big.' She held her hands apart to show Eileen how big Angelika was.

'I thought you were rich,' said Eileen. 'Aren't you rich?'

'No,' said Clara. 'Like other people.'

'I thought all Jews were rich,' said Eileen. 'That's what my Mum said. Aren't all Jews rich?'

Clara was so angry she could feel herself blushing. 'No, some are rich and some are not so rich. Even some are poor.'

'Oh,' said Eileen. Phyllis knew what that meant. It meant: that's what you say, but I don't

67

believe you. She tried to change the subject:

'Wasn't *Silent Night* good in German, Eileen? You sang it ever so well, Clara. Didn't she sing it ever so well?'

'Yes,' said Eileen. 'It's jolly clever of you, Clara, to know all the words. As it's a Christian song, I mean.'

Clara said: 'I have many friends in school who are not Jewish. My best friend, Marianne . . .' she stopped.

'What about her?' Eileen asked.

Clara could see that Phyllis was looking anxious. What good would it do to try and explain things to Eileen? It was better to keep quiet. At least Phyllis wouldn't be worried.

'It doesn't matter,' Clara said. 'Let us arrange this lovely dolls' house.'

The girls played weddings with the dolls; then they played banquets.

'Phyllis and I,' Eileen said, 'will dress everyone, and Clara, you can lay the table. All the table stuff is in that box over there.'

Phyllis kept looking at Clara to see how she was getting on. It was hard to know how to behave. Either Eileen or Clara could easily be offended if it looked as though she were taking sides. She felt as though she was walking along the top of a very narrow wall. She pushed a doll's arms into a jacket and buttoned it up. When all the dolls were ready for the banquet, she and Eileen brought them back and began to arrange them round the table.

'Golly, you've done it all ever so well, Clara! Hasn't she, Eileen? Isn't the table lovely?' Eileen had to concede it was.

'Well done,' she said. 'It's jolly grand. Where did you find the little candelabra? It's been lost for ages. My mum brought it back from London for me, and she was ever so cross with me when I lost it.'

'It was in one of the toy cupboards. I open it and find the candelabra. Is pretty, yes?'

'Yes, it's lovely,' Phyllis said. 'Now the table looks like a proper banqueting table.'

'Let's start the game, then,' said Eileen. 'I'll be the beautiful Duchess Belinda.'

· 7 ·

Sunday, 18th December, 1938

At Night

Phyllis woke up suddenly, and looked around her bedroom. Since Clara and Maxi's arrival, her mother had been leaving the bathroom light on, so that Maxi wouldn't be scared in the dark, and this meant that her room was full of shadows she wasn't quite expecting. What had made her wake up so abruptly? Phyllis lay in her bed and listened. What was that noise? Was there a noise? Perhaps she was imagining it. Perhaps she had had a bad dream. No, there was definitely *something*, but Phyllis couldn't think what it was. It didn't sound like burglars . . . it was more like someone sniffing. She wondered whether she ought to wake her parents. They'd be jolly angry with her if all it turned out to be was a dripping tap or something. I'll go out on to the landing, she thought, and listen from there. She pushed back the covers and stood up. She put on her slippers and her dressing gown and wondered why she wasn't screaming with terror. It isn't a frightening noise, she told herself, and that's why I'm going to see what's making it . . . it's a very small noise. Maybe it's a mouse. Phyllis crept on to the landing and stood there, listening as hard as she could. The noise was in Clara and Maxi's room. It sounded just like . . . no, it couldn't possibly be . . . but it sounded just like someone crying, and hiding under the bedclothes. Maybe Maxi was awake, and missing his mum. Phyllis tiptoed to the open door and peeped into the room. She could see Maxi's bed. He was fast asleep, looking just like a little cherub.

'Clara?' Phyllis whispered. 'Clara, is that you? It's me, Phyllis.'

'Hello, Phyllis,' said Clara, also whispering. 'Why are you awake?'

'I heard a noise.' Phyllis made her way to Clara's bed and sat down. 'Clara, have you been crying?'

Phyllis could hardly believe that this sniffly, red-eyed, wild-haired person was the Clara she knew, who had always been so calm, except for the time when Maxi was lost. But they'd all been frantic then, even Mrs Goodison. Could Clara be so sad because of something that she, Phyllis, had done? Or hadn't done? Should she have taken Clara's side more, about all the *Silent Night* business?

Clara sniffed. 'I do not wish that anybody should hear. I do not wish to wake you, Phyllis. I am very sorry.'

'I don't mind,' said Phyllis. 'I didn't know what the noise was . . . Clara, why are you sad?'

'It's hard to say . . . in English.'

'Do try, though,' Phyllis said. 'My dad says you always feel better if you tell someone.'

'This my mother is also saying, so I tell you. It is not one thing. It is many things. Suddenly, I am sick for home.'

'Homesick.'

'Yes. Homesick. Because of what we play with Eileen. When I find the little candelabra, it reminds me of our Menorah.'

'What's that?' Phyllis asked.

'It is for nine candles a candelabra. You have to light one for each night of Hannukah, and after a week, all the candles are shining together.'

'That sounds lovely,' said Phyllis. 'It must look so pretty.'

'Yes,' said Clara. 'We do it every year.'

'Why does it make you cry though?'

'Because this year, we cannot do it. They threw our Menorah into the street, those terrible men. And also because Maxi and I are here, and Mama is there, and Papa is not with us, but in Dachau, and because I am bad, bad. I have forgot that today is the first day of Hannukah, and instead I sing *Stille Nacht* in German!' Clara began to sob with all her heart, and flung herself face down on her pillow. Phyllis didn't know what to do. Nobody had ever looked to her for that kind of help before. Should she go and wake Mum and Dad? She patted Clara on the back, tentatively.

'Ssh!' she said. 'You'll wake Maxi. Clara, sit up. Listen. It's all right. It'll be all right. Do sit up.' Clara sniffed and turned to face Phyllis.

'I'm sorry,' she said. 'You are so kind. It is wrong for me to cry.'

Phyllis threw her arms around Clara and hugged her tight.

'No it jolly well isn't wrong. You must miss

your mum and dad dreadfully. I know I would. It wouldn't be the same thing at all, someone else being nice to you, however kind they were . . . only don't worry about *Silent Night*. If you tell Miss Pea you feel funny singing it, she won't make you. Honestly. I'll come and tell her with you, if you like. And I've had a good idea.'

'What?'

Phyllis stopped hugging Clara and stood up.

'Put on your dressing gown and follow me downstairs. Be as quiet as you can.'

'What are we going to do?'

'You'll see. Hurry.'

Phyllis and Clara made their way downstairs. They went through the kitchen, into the pantry, and turned on the light. Clara watched silently as Phyllis fetched a saucer and a box of matches.

'I know where Mum keeps the candles,' she said. 'If I give you one, and you light it, you can say a special prayer for . . . whatever it's called.'

'Hannukah,' Clara whispered.

'Yes.' Phyllis went to the drawer where the candles were kept, and took one out.

'Here,' she said to Clara. 'Will this do?'

'Thank you,' said Clara and she lit the thick white candle Phyllis had given her. She let some drops of wax fall on to the saucer and stuck the candle into them, so that it stood upright. The small flame leapt upwards. Phyllis smiled and listened as her friend said some strange words in a language she didn't recognize.

'What is Hannukah, Clara?' she asked. 'Is it a bit like Christmas?'

'No,' said Clara. 'Not really, except that it's a festival for winter. At Hannukah we remember a miracle. The Jews were fighting someone . . . their leader was called Judah Maccabee, and there was only enough oil in their lamps for one night of lamplight. But God made the oil last for eight days. We light candles for each night that the oil burned in the lamps.'

'Are you feeling better now?' she asked.

'Yes,' said Clara. 'Much better. Let's go to bed now.'

'Shall we take the candle?' Phyllis asked.

'No,' said Clara. 'Let it stay here. I blow it out now, and I light it again tomorrow for a few minutes, and again, each night of Hannukah.' She puffed at the flame, and it went out at once. A thin trail of blueish smoke hung in the air.

'Is it all right to have just one?' Phyllis asked. 'If you're supposed to have nine?'

'One is enough,' said Clara. 'It will shine for all the other candles, also. The ones we haven't got. It will be enough. Tomorrow I will tell you about all the good things we eat at Hannukah . . . doughnuts and potato cakes.'

'Don't!' said Phyllis. 'I'm starving, and there aren't any doughnuts. We could have a ginger biscuit if you like.' Phyllis and Clara took a biscuit each out of the tin on the top shelf of the pantry.

'I'll hide the candle in the cupboard till tomorrow,' said Phyllis, 'and I'll tell Mum and Dad about Hannukah in time for tomorrow night.'

The girls crept silently up to their bedrooms again.

· 8 ·

20th December, 1938

The Nativity Play

Phyllis and Eileen were watching everything from the wings at the right-hand side of the stage. All the children were ready in their costumes. Eileen's white wings and golden halo made her look prettier than ever. Phyllis wished that the Innkeeper's Wife could have been allowed to wear something a little more interesting than a long, brown frock cut down from some old parent's dress.

'Don't the infants look sweet?' she whispered. Maxi was the sweetest of all, Phyllis thought. He had on what looked like a white fluffy bathing suit. All the lambs wore pink false ears and lots of cotton wool curls on their heads. They were skipping about with excitement saying 'Baa-aa' over and over again.

The lights went out in the hall. All the parents and grandparents and brothers and sisters sat in the dark and waited for the Nativity play to begin. First, though, Miss Pea had to say a few words. She always did, every year, and everyone was used to it. They knew, each year, exactly what these words would be: thank you to all the children, to the parents for their help with the costumes and props, and 'to my colleague, Mrs Goodison for her sterling work on the pianoforte.'

Everyone clapped as Miss Pea made her way up to the stage.

'Here she comes,' said Eileen. 'We'll be starting soon.'

'Good evening, ladies and gentlemen,' said Miss Pea. 'It's a pleasure to welcome you all to the Long Easterby Nativity play once again. This year, before the play begins, we have a surprise for you. Mr and Mrs Baird, as you know, have offered their hospitality to two young German children. The little boy, Maxi, will be joining our infants in the play, but first his sister, Clara, would like to say something. Clara?'

Clara stepped out from behind the curtain and came to stand beside Miss Pea.

'What's she going to do?' Eileen whispered.

'Someone told me she wasn't going to do *Silent Night*.'

'Ssh!' said Phyllis. 'Let's listen.'

Clara said: 'Good evening. My name is Clara Nussbaum. Maxi is my brother and we are Jewish children. Today is one of the days of Hannukah, the Festival of Lights, so I sing a Hannukah song. Thank you.'

Clara sang the song with no accompaniment. Her clear voice, the foreign words, the unfamiliar tune, rose up and up into the high ceiling, and everyone listened quietly. Phyllis felt tears coming into her eyes. She didn't understand what the words meant, but the tune was filled with longing and sweetness, like a lullaby, and it made her feel sad.

'I don't see,' Eileen whispered, 'what this has got to do with the Nativity, do you? I've never heard of Hannu-whatever it's called.'

'Oh, shut up, Eileen and don't be so beastly!' Phyllis hissed back. Suddenly, she no longer cared whether or not Eileen was her best friend. 'Jesus knew what Hannukah was and so do I! So there! I expect his family celebrated it. I expect

they had doughnuts and potato cakes and everything.' The part about the doughnuts didn't
sound very likely, but she didn't care. Phyllis
wanted Eileen to keep quiet and listen to Clara's
song. When it was over, everybody in the hall
clapped and clapped. They didn't seem to want to
stop, ever. In the end, Miss Pea had to go and
make ssshing noises at them, as though they were
a class of naughty children. Finally the applause
stopped, and the play began.

The next day, the postman brought a postcard for Clara and Maxi.

'Look!' Clara said to Phyllis. 'My father has come home, to our house. He is not any more in the camp. They have a visa and a passport and they come. They say: on the fifteenth of January they come here, to England. They will come.'

Phyllis could see that all the other smiles she had ever seen on Clara's face were a kind of pretend. This smile was so happy that every bit of her face looked quite different. Phyllis said: 'That's the best Christmas present in the world for you and Maxi, isn't it? I'm really happy for you, Clara!' And I am, Phyllis thought. I *am* really happy, only it means Clara and Maxi will probably be leaving, and then I'll be sad. I won't think about it now, she decided. Not yet. Maybe the Nussbaums would settle near Long Easterby and she would still see Clara at school. Nothing, Phyllis said to herself, was going to spoil Christmas. It was sure to be the very best Christmas ever. She and her parents and someone called Mr Parsons were the only people in the world who knew a wonderful secret: that in one of the cottages on Belbridge Road there was a tiny white-and-ginger tom kitten who was waiting to belong to Maxi and to Clara. Mr Parsons would be bringing him to Yew Tree House at eleven o'clock on Christmas morning.

Afterword

Between December 1938 and August 1939, ten thousand children came to Britain on the Kindertransports. Nine thousand of them never saw their parents again.

Further Reading

Now that you have read **A Candle in the Dark**, you might like to read some other books about the Second World War. You might like to read other novels, true stories, or general information books about the war. Here is a selection of the books available.

Fiction

Nina Bawden   **Carrie's War**,
Puffin Books (1994)

Anne Holm   **I am David**,
Mammoth, Reed Books (1995)

Ian Serraillier   **The Silver Sword**,
Puffin Books (1995)

Ann Turnbull   **Room For a Stranger**,
Walker Books (1996)

Non-fiction

Anne Frank   **The Diary of Anne Frank**, *Macmillan Children's Books, Macmillan (1995)*

Wayne Jackman   **Anne Frank**,
Wayland Books (1992)

Jayne Pettit   **A Time to Fight Back: True Stories of Children's Resistance During World War II**
Macmillan Children's Books, Macmillan (1995)

Marilyn Tolhurst   **Home in the Blitz**,
A & C Black (1996)